ASTEROIDS, COMETS, AND METEORS

Rosalind Mist

QEB Publishing

Words in **bold** can be found in the glossary on page 22.

Copyright © QEB Publishing, Inc. 2008

Published in the United States by
QEB Publishing, Inc.
3 Wrigley, Suite A
Irvine, CA 92618

www.qeb-publishing.com

Library of Congress Control Number:
2008012587

ISBN 978 1 59566 142 5

Printed and bound in China

Author Rosalind Mist
Consultant Terry Jennings
Editor Amanda Askew
Designer Melissa Alaverdy
Picture Researcher Maria Joannou

Publisher Steve Evans
Creative Director Zeta Davies

Picture credits
(fc=front cover, t=top, b=bottom, l=left,
r=right, c=centre)

Corbis Sanford/Agliolo 1b, Bryan Allen
20–21, Dennis di Cicco 12r, Sanford/Agliolo
17b, Reuters/Ali Jarekji 18–19

ESA 10l, 12l, 14tl, 14tr

Getty Images John Thys/AFP 20b,
NASA 17t

NASA fc, 15b, HiRISE, MRO, LPL (U Arizona)
23, JPL 14br, JPL/MSSS 7t, JPL-Caltech 14bl,
NSSDC 6t, 15t, Stephen Ostro et al (JPL)/
Arecibo Radio Telescope/NSF 7b

Science Photo Library Roger Harris 1t,
Mike Agliolo 1c, Detlev Van Ravenswaay 8–9,
Mike Agliolo 10–11, Gordon Garradd 13c,
John Foster 16, NASA 20t, Rev Ronald Royer
13l, 13r, Roger Harris 2–3, 6b

Shutterstock 4l, 4–5

Tamas Ladanyi 11r

Contents

The Solar System

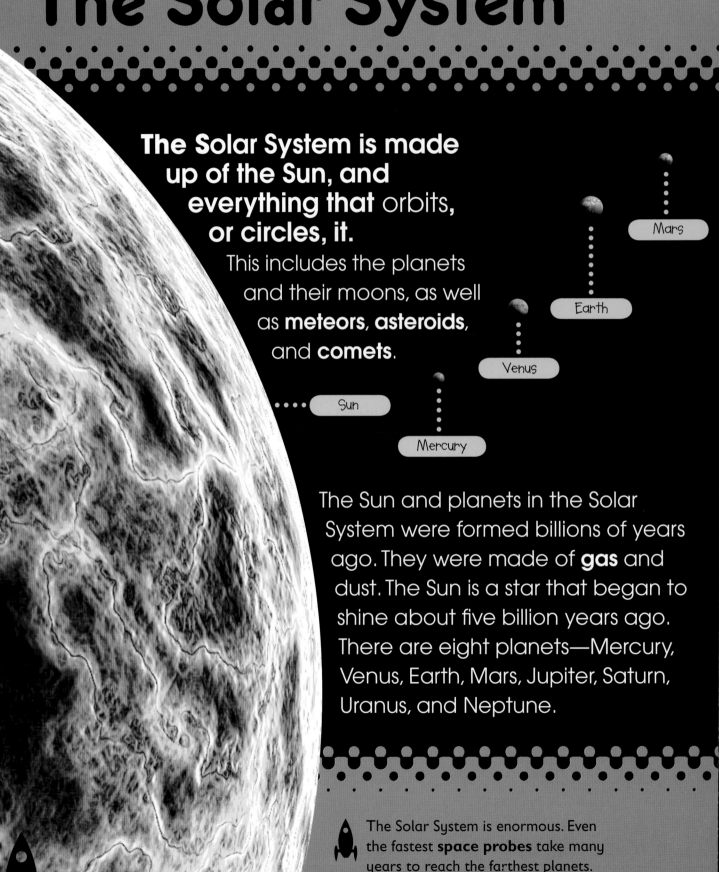

The Solar System is made up of the Sun, and everything that orbits, **or circles, it.** This includes the planets and their moons, as well as **meteors, asteroids,** and **comets**.

Mars

Earth

Venus

Sun

Mercury

The Sun and planets in the Solar System were formed billions of years ago. They were made of **gas** and dust. The Sun is a star that began to shine about five billion years ago. There are eight planets—Mercury, Venus, Earth, Mars, Jupiter, Saturn, Uranus, and Neptune.

The Solar System is enormous. Even the fastest **space probes** take many years to reach the farthest planets.

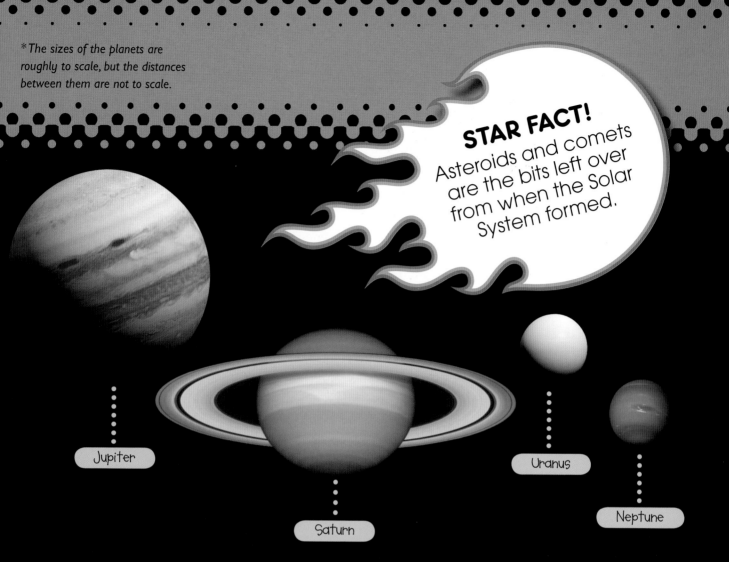

STAR FACT!
Asteroids and comets are the bits left over from when the Solar System formed.

Jupiter

Saturn

Uranus

Neptune

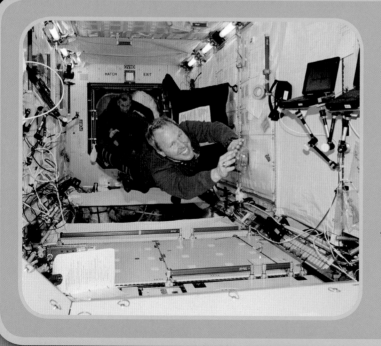

The Solar System is held together by an invisible force called **gravity**. On Earth, gravity stops people from floating into space!

 In the **International Space Station**, the **astronauts** feel weightless because they are falling freely as they orbit the Earth.

Asteroids

Asteroids are large lumps of icy rock or metal moving around the Sun.

More than 200 years ago, **astronomers** were looking for a new planet when they found the first asteroids. These asteroids are between Mars and Jupiter— in the **Asteroid Belt**.

Gaspra was the first asteroid to be seen close-up by a space probe. It is about 5 miles (18 kilometers) long and 6 miles (10 kilometers) across.

Asteroids often orbit together in groups. Even though there are lots of them, they are much farther apart than you might think.

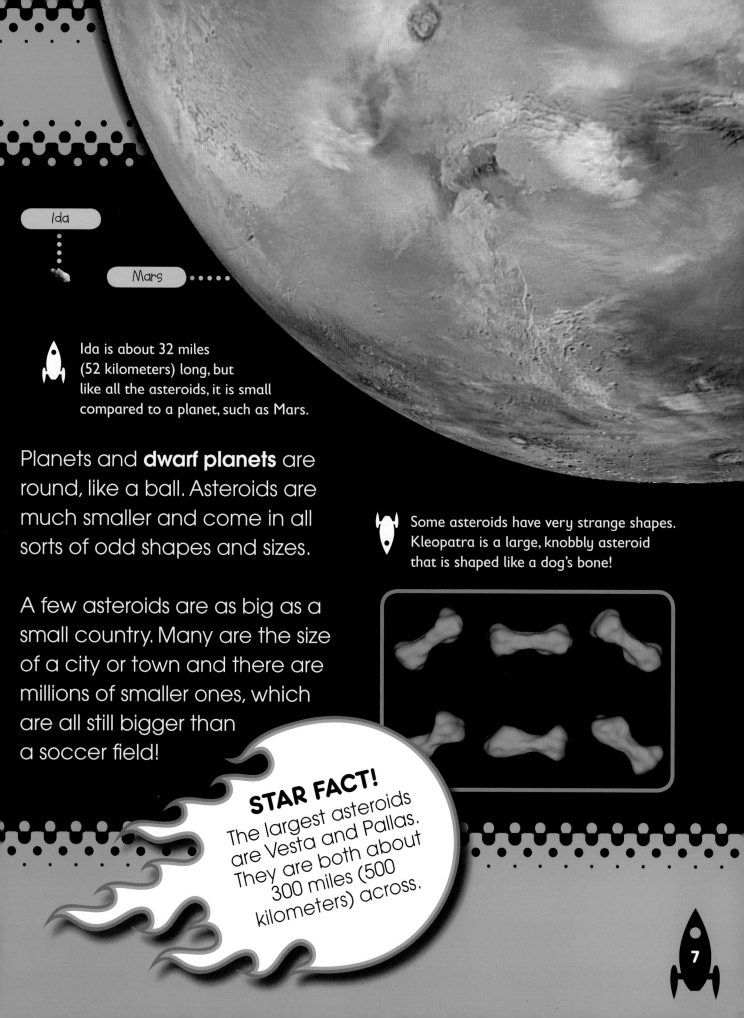

Ida

Mars

Ida is about 32 miles (52 kilometers) long, but like all the asteroids, it is small compared to a planet, such as Mars.

Planets and **dwarf planets** are round, like a ball. Asteroids are much smaller and come in all sorts of odd shapes and sizes.

Some asteroids have very strange shapes. Kleopatra is a large, knobbly asteroid that is shaped like a dog's bone!

A few asteroids are as big as a small country. Many are the size of a city or town and there are millions of smaller ones, which are all still bigger than a soccer field!

STAR FACT!
The largest asteroids are Vesta and Pallas. They are both about 300 miles (500 kilometers) across.

The Asteroid Belt

There are lots of asteroids in the Solar System and most are found in groups, such as the Asteroid Belt between Mars and Jupiter.

Most of the asteroids in the Solar System can be found in the Asteroid Belt. More than one million of them are larger than 0.5 miles (one kilometer)— as large as ten soccer fields. There are millions of smaller asteroids, too. The dwarf planet Ceres was the first object to be found in the Asteroid Belt.

STAR FACT!

If an asteroid gets too close to a planet, it can begin to orbit, or circle, the planet as a moon. Scientists think that the moons of Mars are asteroids from the Asteroid Belt.

Earth

Sun

Mars

Asteroid Belt

Jupiter

 The Asteroid Belt is between Mars and Jupiter. It contains millions of asteroids.

Comets

A comet is like a giant dirty snowball, the size of a town or city. It is made of ice, dust, and small pieces of rock.

As a comet gets closer to the Sun, it starts to melt. It becomes surrounded by lots of gas and dust. As the comet moves, the dust and gas stretch away from it. This is the comet's tail.

 Gas and dust stream from a comet, creating its tail.

A comet's tail can stretch for millions of miles across the Solar System.

STAR FACT!

Comets actually have two tails. In the second tail, gas is blown away by wind from the Sun. It is often quite difficult to see.

From Earth, a comet usually looks like a fuzzy splat in the sky, and it can also have a long tail. You can see comets for a few weeks. As they move slowly across the sky, their tails change length and direction.

Tail

 Comets look fuzzy because they are surrounded by gas and dust. In 2007, Comet Holmes looked like a huge jellyfish in the sky.

Famous comets

Comets often appear reguarly, but the best ones are unexpected.
They grow bright, spectacular tails that can stretch across the sky. After a few weeks, they fade away.

The most famous comet is Halley's Comet. It appears every 75 to 76 years. People have seen this comet for more than 2,000 years. Its orbit takes it out about as far as Pluto.

Great comets

Comet Hale-Bopp
....
Last seen: 1997

Special features:
It had two clearly visible tails.

 Halley's Comet was last seen in 1986 and it will be back again in 2061.

Comet Hyakutake

Last seen: 1996

Special features:
It had an amazing tail.

Comet McNaught

Last seen: 2007

Special features:
It was so bright that you could see it during the day.

Comet West

Last seen: 1976

Special features:
It will not be back for more than 500,000 years.

Edmond Halley (1656-1742)

Halley was an English **scientist**. He thought the comets that were seen in 1531, 1607, and 1682 were very similar and realized that they were the same comet. He believed that it would be seen in 1758—and he was right!

Exploration

To learn more about comets and asteroids, scientists have sent space probes to visit them.
Last time Halley's Comet came close to Earth, the *Giotto* space probe flew close by to see what it looked like. The comet was dark with bright jets of dust and gas.

Halley's Comet

Giotto space probe

 The *Giotto* space probe saw bright jets of gas coming from Halley's dark core, or middle.

The *Stardust* **spacecraft** flew through the tail of Comet Wild 2 and collected dust. The dust was brought back to Earth.

Comet Wild 2

Comet Wild 2

Stardust spacecraft

 The *Stardust* spacecraft has helped scientists to find out what comets are made of.

The *Galileo* space probe was the first to take a close-up picture of an asteroid. It also found an asteroid that has a tiny moon.

Spacecraft have even landed on an asteroid. The Japanese spacecraft *Hayabusa* has collected samples of rock and metal from an asteroid. It will bring it back to Earth in 2010.

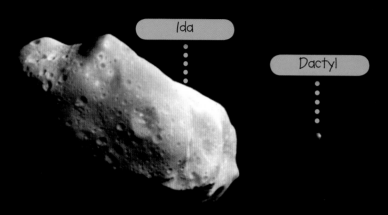

Ida

Dactyl

Ida is an asteroid with its own moon called Dactyl. The moon is about one mile (1.5 kilometers) across.

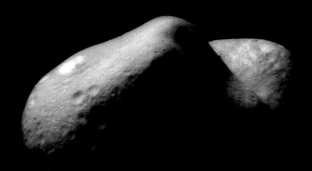

The *NEAR* space probe took many photographs of the Eros asteroid. In 2001, the space probe also landed on its surface.

Stardust

Scientists use a gel to catch dust in space. Ask an adult to help you make jell-O—use more water than the packet says. Let the jell-O nearly set and drop in some hard candy. Did they fall to the bottom or stop halfway?

Meteors

As well as large asteroids, there are lots of other smaller pieces of rock, metal, and dust in the Solar System.
Small pieces, the size of grains of sand, are hitting the Earth's **atmosphere** all the time.

 Meteors shoot quickly across the sky. They appear out of nowhere, burn brightly and then disappear suddenly.

When small pieces of rock and metal hit the atmosphere, they are moving very fast. As they travel through the thick atmosphere, they get very hot and glow. They are called meteors.

STAR FACT!
Some meteors are fast, some are slow. Some are bright, others are dim. Some are colored, and some even explode!

Meteors get so hot that they burn up in the atmosphere. At night, you can see them. The burning meteors look like fast streaks of light in the sky. This is why they are sometimes called "shooting stars."

Earth

 Fireballs can sometimes be as bright as the Moon.

Fireballs are very bright meteors. They sometimes leave a trail behind them. The trail can hang in the sky for a few seconds.

Meteor

 Meteors are about 60 miles (100 kilometers) above the Earth and travel at up to 40 miles (70 kilometers) a second.

Meteor showers

If the Earth passes through or near the dusty trail left by a comet, we see more meteors than normal. This is called a meteor shower.

Meteor showers occur around the same time every year. As meteor showers come from different comets, each shower is slightly different.

The best showers to see are the Perseids from July 17 to August 24, and the Geminids from December 7 to 13.

STAR FACT!
Meteor showers are named after the star **constellation** in the sky where the meteors seem to come from.

Looking for meteors

· · · · · · · · · · · · · · · ·

The sky needs to be dark with no Moon, and you need to be away from bright lights. If you can see lots of stars, you should be able to see meteors. Meteors move quickly across the sky and only a few are bright. Expect to see two or three in 20 minutes.

 In a meteor storm, the meteors are bright and cut across the trails left by stars.

Meteorites

A large meteor might not completely burn up in the Earth's atmosphere.
If it hits the ground, it is called a **meteorite**. There are two types of meteorite—stony and iron.

 An iron meteorite was found on the surface of Mars. It was the size of a basketball.

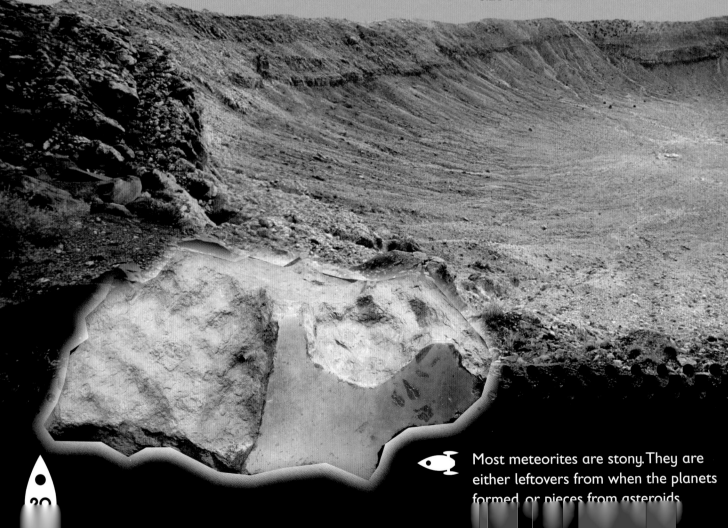

Most meteorites are stony. They are either leftovers from when the planets formed, or pieces from asteroids.

Rocky moons and planets, such as Mars, have lots of **craters**. Craters are the holes left by large meteorites.

The meteorite that made Earth's Meteor Crater was about 160 feet (50 meters) across. Astronomers are looking for new asteroids to try to make sure one does not catch us by surprise!

Meteor Crater in Arizona, is nearly one mile (1,200 meters) wide and 600 feet (180 meters) deep. Although it is a very large dent in the ground, it is still smaller than craters on the Moon.

STAR FACT!
Scientists think that some meteorites are rocks that were knocked off Mars and have traveled through space before reaching Earth.

Glossary

Asteroid
A large lump of rock, too small to be a planet or dwarf planet.

Asteroid Belt
Area between Mars and Jupiter where there are lots of asteroids.

Astronaut
A person who travels in space.

Astronomer
A scientist who studies the Solar System, stars, and galaxies.

Atmosphere
A layer of gases around a planet or moon.

Comet
An object in space made of rock and ice.

Constellation
A named group of stars.

Crater
A hole made on the surface of a planet or moon by an asteroid or comet.

Dwarf planet
A rocky body that is larger than an asteroid, but too small to be a planet.

Gas
A substance, such as air, that is not solid or liquid. Gas cannot usually be seen.

Gravity
Attractive pulling force between any massive objects.

International Space Station
Large space laboratory where astronauts can live for months.

Meteor
A glowing trail in the sky left by a small piece of rock from space.

Meteorite
A piece of rock or metal from space that has reached the ground.

Orbit
The path of one body around another, such as a planet around the Sun.

Scientist
A person who studies science.

Spacecraft
A vehicle that travels in space.

Space probe
A spacecraft without people on board.

Index

The term asteroid refers to a large rocky body, usually more than one mile across. Some definitions state that an object larger than 160 feet (50 meters) across is an asteroid. Bodies that are smaller, such as boulders, rocks, and sand-sized particles are called meteoroids. Particles that are even smaller are micro-meteoroids and interplanetary dust.

 Your eyes get better at seeing in the dark after about 20 minutes. Look halfway up the sky. It is easier on your neck if you can lie down, but make sure you don't get cold.

 The most reliable meteor shower is the Perseid shower, which is active from late July through most of August each year, peaking around August 12. You can see one Perseid meteor each minute on average. See meteorshowersonline.com* for more general information and details of other meteor showers.

*Website information is correct at time of going to press. However, the publishers cannot accept liability for any information or links found on third-party websites.

 Occasionally, the Earth passes through a very dusty part of a comet's orbit and we see so many meteors that it really does seem like they are raining down. This is a meteor storm. The Leonids, which occur around November 16 to 17, are known for their spectacular storms, but they only occur every 33 years.

 The aim of the *Stardust* mission was to capture cometary and interplanetary dust. When the dust met the spacecraft, it was traveling extremely fast—up to six times the speed of a bullet. To slow the particles gradually without damaging them, *Stardust* used a very low density aerogel. This "solid blue smoke" is 99.8 percent empty space. The particles embedded themselves in the gel at the end of long visible tracks.